This Journal Belongs To

_____

Created by Arielle Haughee

ORANGE BLOSSOM
PUBLISHING

Maitland, Florida

© 2020 by Arielle Haughee.
All rights reserved. No part of this book may be transmitted in any form or by any means, electronic or mechanical, including photocopying, recording, or by any information storage or retrieval system, in part, in any form, without the permission of the publisher.

Published 2020 by Orange Blossom Publishing
Maitland, Florida
www.orangeblossombooks.com

ISBN: 978-1-949935-17-2

A Note from Arielle

Being a mother is the most important, most stressful, most all-consuming job you'll ever have. Sometimes it can seem to completely swallow you whole. (I battled post partum depression for a year after both of my boys were born. I remember weeks feeling like I was on a gray carousel with nothing to look forward to.)

You also constantly question if you are doing the right thing, and always thinking you can do more. You bounce back and forth between anxiety and guilt, never taking a step back to appreciate what you've done or how far you've come.

It takes a concerted effort to release the stress and negative thoughts and emotions. Focusing on yourself makes you a better person and a better mom.

The goal with this journal is to help you focus within and to empower you to create peace in your life. Wishing you many days of happiness and serenity.

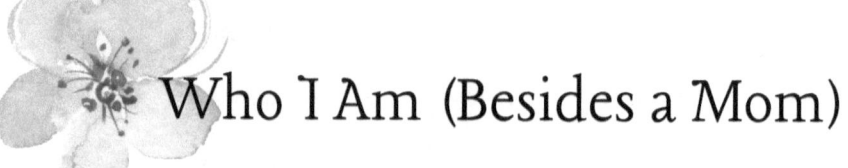

Who I Am (Besides a Mom)

Think about who you are as a total person. Consider your relationships to others (daughter, sister, wife, friend...), your career, your hobbies and skills, spirituality...all the things that make you who you are.

_____
_____
_____
_____
_____
_____
_____
_____
_____
_____
_____
_____
_____
_____
_____
_____
_____
_____
_____
_____

Building My Tribe

Having a group of people that can make you laugh, offer encouragement, and truly understand what it's like to be a parent are essential. Think of a variety of people who could be your support tribe.

Family members:
....
....
....

Current friends:
....
....
....

Acquaintences:
....
....
....

Places/Ideas to meet new mom friends:
....
....
....
....

My Goal Schedule

	Early a.m.	7 - 9 a.m.	9 - 11 a.m.	11 - 1 p.m.
Monday				
Tuesday				
Wednesday				
Thursday				
Friday				
Weekend				

I will fill out this journal on _____
and _____.

1 - 3 p.m.   3 - 5 p.m.   6 - 8 p.m.   9 - 11 p.m.   Late p.m.

My Adjusted Goal Schedule

	Early a.m.	7 - 9 a.m.	9 - 11 a.m.	11 - 1 p.m.
Monday				
Tuesday				
Wednesday				
Thursday				
Friday				
Weekend				

I will fill out this journal on _____
and _____.

1 - 3 p.m.   3 - 5 p.m.   6 - 8 p.m.   9 - 11 p.m.   Late p.m.

My Adjusted Adjusted Goal Schedule

	Early a.m.	7 - 9 a.m.	9 - 11 a.m.	11 - 1 p.m.
Monday				
Tuesday				
Wednesday				
Thursday				
Friday				
Weekend				

I will fill out this journal on _____
and _____.

1 - 3 p.m.   3 - 5 p.m.   6 - 8 p.m.   9 - 11 p.m.   Late p.m.

Mommy Mantras

When I feel anxious, I will tell myself:

When I feel guilty, I will tell myself:

When I feel worried, I will tell myself:

When I feel like a failure, I will tell myself:

Planning for the Week

My focus for this week	Stressors for this week
My break(s) will be on	I won't put myself last for
My social media limit	When I will do my hobby
When I will exercise	I will release anxiety/guilt by

Reflecting on the Week

Something frustrating	Something rewarding

I felt lost when	I felt myself when

I was proud of myself for	I smiled when

I need to let go of	My inner peace level score for this week (1 - 5)

Planning for the Week

My focus for this week	Stressors for this week
My break(s) will be on	I won't put myself last for
My social media limit	When I will do my hobby
When I will exercise	I will release anxiety/guilt by

Reflecting on the Week

Something frustrating	Something rewarding

I felt lost when	I felt myself when

I was proud of myself for	I smiled when

I need to let go of	My inner peace level score for this week: (1 - 5)

Planning for the Week

My focus for this week	Stressors for this week
My break(s) will be on	I won't put myself last for
My social media limit	When I will do my hobby
When I will exercise	I will release anxiety/guilt by

Reflecting on the Week

Something frustrating	Something rewarding

I felt lost when	I felt myself when

I was proud of myself for	I smiled when

I need to let go of	My inner peace level score for this week: (1 - 5)

Planning for the Week

My focus for this week	Stressors for this week
My break(s) will be on	I won't put myself last for
My social media limit	When I will do my hobby
When I will exercise	I will release anxiety/guilt by

Reflecting on the Week

Something frustrating	Something rewarding

I felt lost when	I felt myself when

I was proud of myself for	I smiled when

I need to let go of	My inner peace level score for this week: (1 - 5)

Serenity comes from within.

Monthly Reflection

What was the highest point of the month? Lowest?

Did you remember to say your mantras when you were feeling low?

Do you notice any patterns for when you had negative feelings (triggers, something neglected)?

Do you need to adjust your schedule to give you a better sense of calm?

Go back through the month and reread the third row of each week on the Reflection side. Praise yourself.

No one told me...

There is a lot they don't tell you about motherhood. Think of the good things, the hard things, and the absolutely hilarious things.

Planning for the Week

My focus for this week	Stressors for this week
My break(s) will be on	I won't put myself last for
My social media limit	When I will do my hobby
When I will exercise	I will release anxiety/guilt by

Reflecting on the Week

Something frustrating	Something rewarding

I felt lost when	I felt myself when

I was proud of myself for	I smiled when

I need to let go of	My inner peace level score for this week: (1 - 5)

Planning for the Week

My focus for this week	Stressors for this week
My break(s) will be on	I won't put myself last for
My social media limit	When I will do my hobby
When I will exercise	I will release anxiety/guilt by

Reflecting on the Week

Something frustrating	Something rewarding

I felt lost when	I felt myself when

I was proud of myself for	I smiled when

I need to let go of	My inner peace level score for this week: (1 - 5)

Planning for the Week

My focus for this week	Stressors for this week
My break(s) will be on	I won't put myself last for
My social media limit	When I will do my hobby
When I will exercise	I will release anxiety/guilt by

Reflecting on the Week

Something frustrating	Something rewarding

I felt lost when	I felt myself when

I was proud of myself for	I smiled when

I need to let go of	My inner peace level score for this week (1 - 5)

Planning for the Week

My focus for this week	Stressors for this week
My break(s) will be on	I won't put myself last for
My social media limit	When I will do my hobby
When I will exercise	I will release anxiety/guilt by

Reflecting on the Week

Something frustrating	Something rewarding

I felt lost when	I felt myself when

I was proud of myself for	I smiled when

I need to let go of	My inner peace level score for this week: (1 - 5)

You are doing the most important job in the world.

Monthly Reflection

What was the highest point of the month? Lowest?

Did you remember to say your mantras when you were feeling low?

Do you notice any patterns for when you had negative feelings (triggers, something neglected)?

Do you need to adjust your schedule to give you a better sense of calm?

Go back through the month and reread the third row of each week on the Reflection side. Praise yourself.

A Moment to Remember

Planning for the Week

My focus for this week	Stressors for this week
My break(s) will be on	I won't put myself last for
My social media limit	When I will do my hobby
When I will exercise	I will release anxiety/guilt by

Reflecting on the Week

Something frustrating	Something rewarding
I felt lost when	I felt myself when
I was proud of myself for	I smiled when
I need to let go of	My inner peace level score for this week: (1 - 5)

Planning for the Week

My focus for this week	Stressors for this week
My break(s) will be on	I won't put myself last for
My social media limit	When I will do my hobby
When I will exercise	I will release anxiety/guilt by

Reflecting on the Week

Something frustrating	Something rewarding

I felt lost when	I felt myself when

I was proud of myself for	I smiled when

I need to let go of	My inner peace level score for this week: (1 - 5)

Planning for the Week

My focus for this week	Stressors for this week
My break(s) will be on	I won't put myself last for
My social media limit	When I will do my hobby
When I will exercise	I will release anxiety/guilt by

Reflecting on the Week

Something frustrating	Something rewarding

I felt lost when	I felt myself when

I was proud of myself for	I smiled when

I need to let go of	My inner peace level score for this week (1 - 5)

Planning for the Week

My focus for this week	Stressors for this week
My break(s) will be on	I won't put myself last for
My social media limit	When I will do my hobby
When I will exercise	I will release anxiety/guilt by

Reflecting on the Week

Something frustrating	Something rewarding
I felt lost when	I felt myself when
I was proud of myself for	I smiled when
I need to let go of	My inner peace level score for this week: (1 - 5)

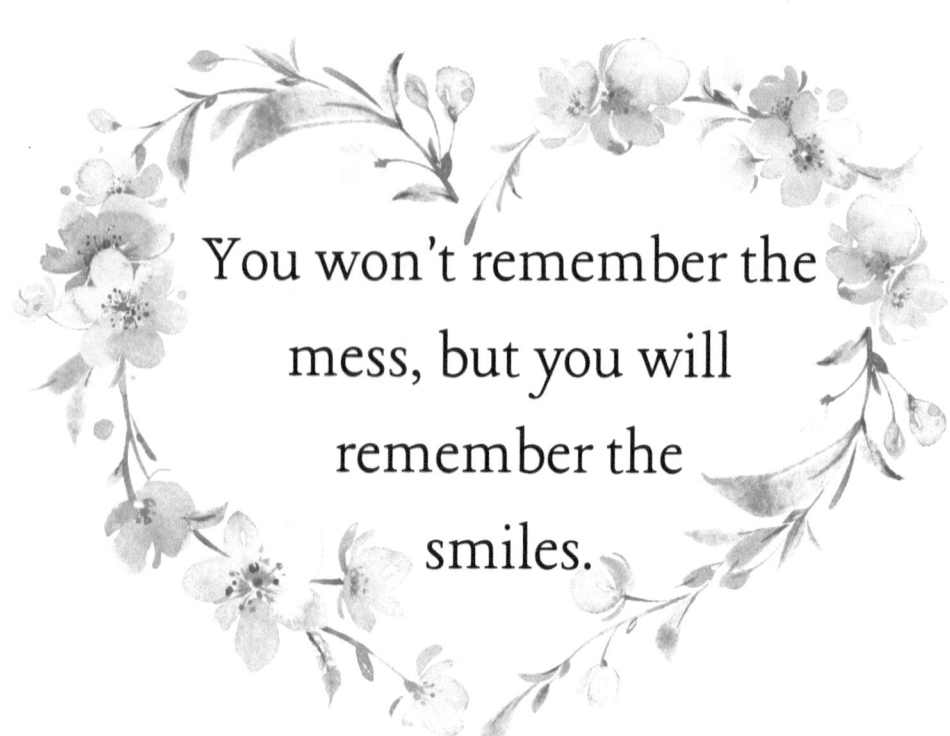

You won't remember the mess, but you will remember the smiles.

Monthly Reflection

What was the highest point of the month? Lowest?

Did you remember to say your mantras when you were feeling low?

Do you notice any patterns for when you had negative feelings (triggers, something neglected)?

Do you need to adjust your schedule to give you a better sense of calm?

Go back through the month and reread the third row of each week on the Reflection side. Praise yourself.

I Forgive Myself

We aren't perfect. No one is. But you shouldn't beat yourself up over mistakes or things that weren't your fault. Take a moment to release some guilt so you can move on.

Planning for the Week

My focus for this week	Stressors for this week
My break(s) will be on	I won't put myself last for
My social media limit	When I will do my hobby
When I will exercise	I will release anxiety/guilt by

Reflecting on the Week

Something frustrating	Something rewarding

I felt lost when	I felt myself when

I was proud of myself for	I smiled when

I need to let go of	My inner peace level score for this week: (1 - 5)

Planning for the Week

My focus for this week	Stressors for this week
My break(s) will be on	I won't put myself last for
My social media limit	When I will do my hobby
When I will exercise	I will release anxiety/guilt by

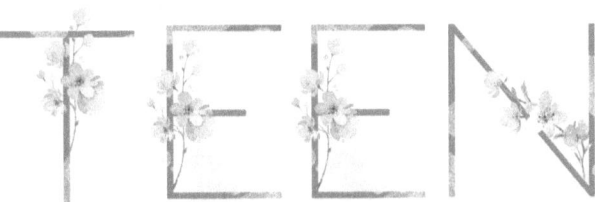

Reflecting on the Week

Something frustrating	Something rewarding
I felt lost when	I felt myself when
I was proud of myself for	I smiled when
I need to let go of	My inner peace level score for this week (1 - 5)

Planning for the Week

My focus for this week	Stressors for this week
My break(s) will be on	I won't put myself last for
My social media limit	When I will do my hobby
When I will exercise	I will release anxiety/guilt by

Reflecting on the Week

Something frustrating	Something rewarding
I felt lost when	I felt myself when
I was proud of myself for	I smiled when
I need to let go of	My inner peace level score for this week: (1 - 5)

Planning for the Week

My focus for this week	Stressors for this week
My break(s) will be on	I won't put myself last for
My social media limit	When I will do my hobby
When I will exercise	I will release anxiety/guilt by

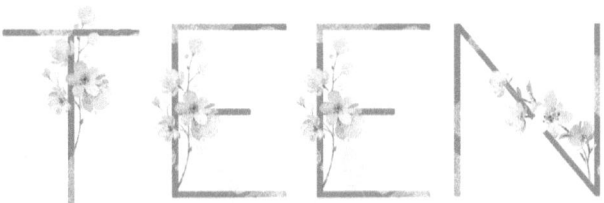

Reflecting on the Week

Something frustrating	Something rewarding
I felt lost when	I felt myself when
I was proud of myself for	I smiled when
I need to let go of	My inner peace level score for this week: (1 - 5)

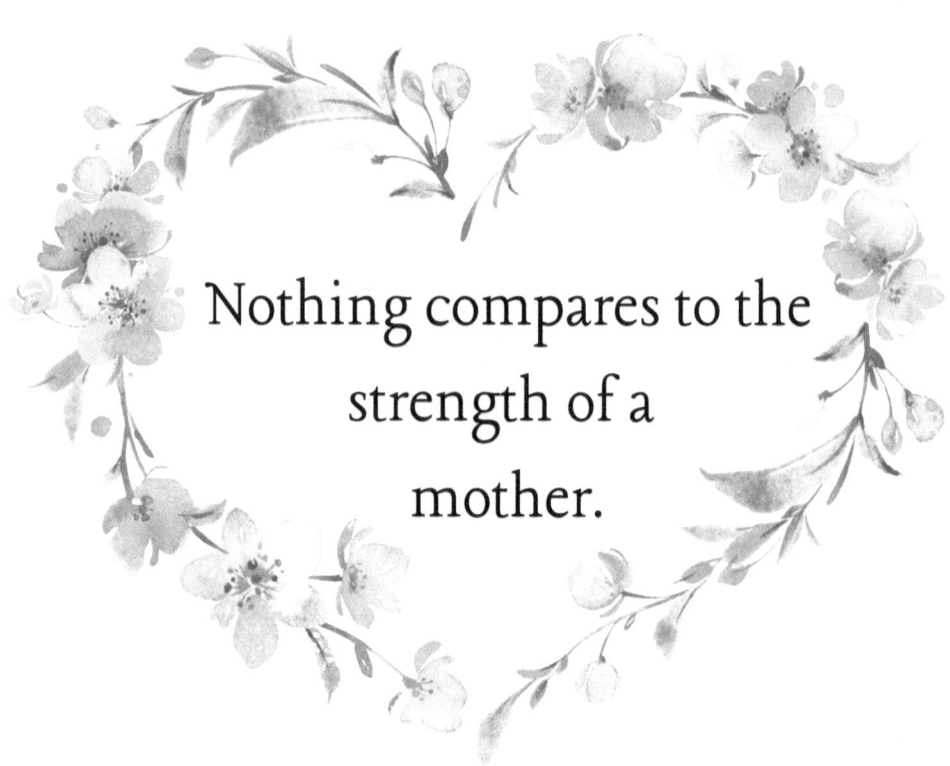

Nothing compares to the strength of a mother.

Monthly Reflection

What was the highest point of the month? Lowest?

Did you remember to say your mantras when you were feeling low?

Do you notice any patterns for when you had negative feelings (triggers, something neglected)?

Do you need to adjust your schedule to give you a better sense of calm?

Go back through the month and reread the third row of each week on the Reflection side. Praise yourself.

Something I Want to Forget

Write the memory on this page. Any time it pops in your head, tell yourself those words are here on this paper and nowhere else. Then refocus.

Planning for the Week

My focus for this week	Stressors for this week
My break(s) will be on	I won't put myself last for
My social media limit	When I will do my hobby
When I will exercise	I will release anxiety/guilt by

Reflecting on the Week

Something frustrating	Something rewarding
I felt lost when	I felt myself when
I was proud of myself for	I smiled when
I need to let go of	My inner peace level score for this week: (1 - 5)

Planning for the Week

My focus for this week	Stressors for this week
My break(s) will be on	I won't put myself last for
My social media limit	When I will do my hobby
When I will exercise	I will release anxiety/guilt by

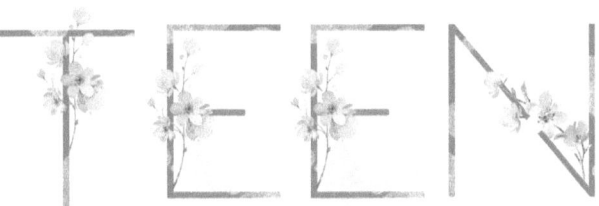

Reflecting on the Week

Something frustrating	Something rewarding

I felt lost when	I felt myself when

I was proud of myself for	I smiled when

I need to let go of	My inner peace level score for this week: (1 - 5)

Planning for the Week

My focus for this week	Stressors for this week

My break(s) will be on	I won't put myself last for

My social media limit	When I will do my hobby

When I will exercise	I will release anxiety/guilt by

Reflecting on the Week

Something frustrating	Something rewarding
I felt lost when	I felt myself when
I was proud of myself for	I smiled when
I need to let go of	My inner peace level score for this week (1 - 5)

Planning for the Week

My focus for this week	Stressors for this week

My break(s) will be on	I won't put myself last for

My social media limit	When I will do my hobby

When I will exercise	I will release anxiety/guilt by

Reflecting on the Week

Something frustrating	Something rewarding

I felt lost when	I felt myself when

I was proud of myself for	I smiled when

I need to let go of	My inner peace level score for this week: (1 - 5)

Self-care makes for a better mom.

Monthly Reflection

What was the highest point of the month? Lowest?

Did you remember to say your mantras when you were feeling low?

Do you notice any patterns for when you had negative feelings (triggers, something neglected)?

Do you need to adjust your schedule to give you a better sense of calm?

Go back through the month and reread the third row of each week on the Reflection side. Praise yourself.

Ways to Integrate Fun

Sometimes it seems like the kids get to have all the fun while we just clean up from it. How can YOU have fun during the day?

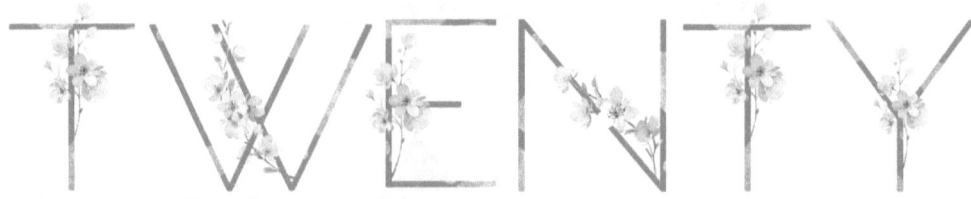

Planning for the Week

My focus for this week	Stressors for this week
My break(s) will be on	I won't put myself last for
My social media limit	When I will do my hobby
When I will exercise	I will release anxiety/guilt by

Reflecting on the Week

Something frustrating	Something rewarding
I felt lost when	I felt myself when
I was proud of myself for	I smiled when
I need to let go of	My inner peace level score for this week: (1 - 5)

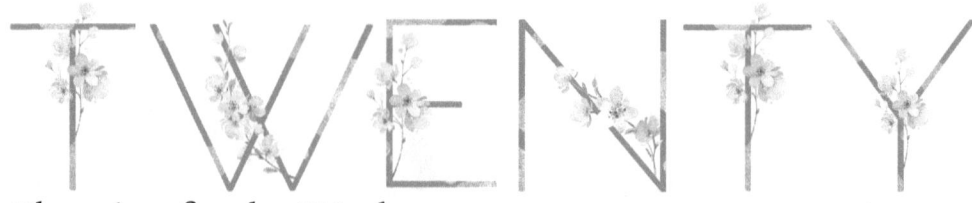

Planning for the Week

My focus for this week	Stressors for this week
My break(s) will be on	I won't put myself last for
My social media limit	When I will do my hobby
When I will exercise	I will release anxiety/guilt by

Reflecting on the Week

Something frustrating	Something rewarding
I felt lost when	I felt myself when
I was proud of myself for	I smiled when
I need to let go of	My inner peace level score for this week: (1 - 5)

Planning for the Week

My focus for this week	Stressors for this week
My break(s) will be on	I won't put myself last for
My social media limit	When I will do my hobby
When I will exercise	I will release anxiety/guilt by

Reflecting on the Week

Something frustrating	Something rewarding

I felt lost when	I felt myself when

I was proud of myself for	I smiled when

I need to let go of	My inner peace level score for this week: (1 - 5)

Planning for the Week

My focus for this week	Stressors for this week
My break(s) will be on	I won't put myself last for
My social media limit	When I will do my hobby
When I will exercise	I will release anxiety/guilt by

Reflecting on the Week

Something frustrating	Something rewarding
I felt lost when	I felt myself when
I was proud of myself for	I smiled when
I need to let go of	My inner peace level score for this week (1 - 5)

The hard times only make you stronger.

Monthly Reflection

What was the highest point of the month? Lowest?

Did you remember to say your mantras when you were feeling low?

Do you notice any patterns for when you had negative feelings (triggers, something neglected)?

Do you need to adjust your schedule to give you a better sense of calm?

Go back through the month and reread the third row of each week on the Reflection side. Praise yourself.

Ideas for a Mental Escape

It's easy to feel trapped in the house or at work or in your life in general. How can you have a mental escape for yourself? Some ideas include books, TV series, art...

Planning for the Week

My focus for this week	Stressors for this week
My break(s) will be on	I won't put myself last for
My social media limit	When I will do my hobby
When I will exercise	I will release anxiety/guilt by

Reflecting on the Week

Something frustrating	Something rewarding
I felt lost when	I felt myself when
I was proud of myself for	I smiled when
I need to let go of	My inner peace level score for this week: (1 - 5)

Planning for the Week

My focus for this week	Stressors for this week
My break(s) will be on	I won't put myself last for
My social media limit	When I will do my hobby
When I will exercise	I will release anxiety/guilt by

Reflecting on the Week

Something frustrating	Something rewarding
I felt lost when	I felt myself when
I was proud of myself for	I smiled when
I need to let go of	My inner peace level score for this week: (1 - 5)

Planning for the Week

My focus for this week	Stressors for this week
My break(s) will be on	I won't put myself last for
My social media limit	When I will do my hobby
When I will exercise	I will release anxiety/guilt by

SEVEN

Reflecting on the Week

Something frustrating	Something rewarding
I felt lost when	I felt myself when
I was proud of myself for	I smiled when
I need to let go of	My inner peace level score for this week: (1 - 5)

Planning for the Week

My focus for this week	Stressors for this week
My break(s) will be on	I won't put myself last for
My social media limit	When I will do my hobby
When I will exercise	I will release anxiety/guilt by

EIGHT

Reflecting on the Week

Something frustrating	Something rewarding

I felt lost when	I felt myself when

I was proud of myself for	I smiled when

I need to let go of	My inner peace level score for this week: (1 - 5)

You are building the future everyday.

Monthly Reflection

What was the highest point of the month? Lowest?

Did you remember to say your mantras when you were feeling low?

Do you notice any patterns for when you had negative feelings (triggers, something neglected)?

Do you need to adjust your schedule to give you a better sense of calm?

Go back through the month and reread the third row of each week on the Reflection side. Praise yourself.

Putting on Your Battle Gear

When you know you have a tough day ahead, think about what you can do to mentally steel yourself. What is your battle gear? You can wear clothes that make you feel confident, get that special cup of coffee first thing, or play music to pump you up. Brainstorm ideas to make you feel empowered to take on the challenge ahead.

Planning for the Week

My focus for this week	Stressors for this week
My break(s) will be on	I won't put myself last for
My social media limit	When I will do my hobby
When I will exercise	I will release anxiety/guilt by

Reflecting on the Week

Something frustrating	Something rewarding
I felt lost when	I felt myself when
I was proud of myself for	I smiled when
I need to let go of	My inner peace level score for this week: (1 - 5)

Planning for the Week

My focus for this week	Stressors for this week
My break(s) will be on	I won't put myself last for
My social media limit	When I will do my hobby
When I will exercise	I will release anxiety/guilt by

Reflecting on the Week

Something frustrating	Something rewarding
I felt lost when	I felt myself when
I was proud of myself for	I smiled when
I need to let go of	My inner peace level score for this week: (1 - 5)

Planning for the Week

My focus for this week	Stressors for this week

My break(s) will be on	I won't put myself last for

My social media limit	When I will do my hobby

When I will exercise	I will release anxiety/guilt by

Reflecting on the Week

Something frustrating	Something rewarding

I felt lost when	I felt myself when

I was proud of myself for	I smiled when

I need to let go of	My inner peace level score for this week: (1 - 5)

Planning for the Week

My focus for this week	Stressors for this week
My break(s) will be on	I won't put myself last for
My social media limit	When I will do my hobby
When I will exercise	I will release anxiety/guilt by

Reflecting on the Week

Something frustrating	Something rewarding
I felt lost when	I felt myself when
I was proud of myself for	I smiled when
I need to let go of	My inner peace level score for this week: (1 - 5)

There is magic in the memories.

Monthly Reflection

What was the highest point of the month? Lowest?

Did you remember to say your mantras when you were feeling low?

Do you notice any patterns for when you had negative feelings (triggers, something neglected)?

Do you need to adjust your schedule to give you a better sense of calm?

Go back through the month and reread the third row of each week on the Reflection side. Praise yourself.

Meditation Time

When can you give yourself a few minutes of quiet time to focus inward and release stress? Look at your schedule and see where you can fit it in. Think about where you will be and what mantras you will say.

Planning for the Week

My focus for this week	Stressors for this week
My break(s) will be on	I won't put myself last for
My social media limit	When I will do my hobby
When I will exercise	I will release anxiety/guilt by

Reflecting on the Week

Something frustrating	Something rewarding
I felt lost when	I felt myself when
I was proud of myself for	I smiled when
I need to let go of	My inner peace level score for this week (1 - 5)

Planning for the Week

My focus for this week	Stressors for this week
My break(s) will be on	I won't put myself last for
My social media limit	When I will do my hobby
When I will exercise	I will release anxiety/guilt by

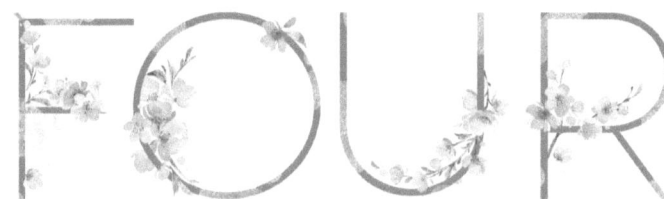

Reflecting on the Week

Something frustrating	Something rewarding
I felt lost when	I felt myself when
I was proud of myself for	I smiled when
I need to let go of	My inner peace level score for this week: (1 - 5)

Planning for the Week

My focus for this week	Stressors for this week

My break(s) will be on	I won't put myself last for

My social media limit	When I will do my hobby

When I will exercise	I will release anxiety/guilt by

Reflecting on the Week

Something frustrating	Something rewarding
I felt lost when	I felt myself when
I was proud of myself for	I smiled when
I need to let go of	My inner peace level score for this week (1 - 5)

Planning for the Week

My focus for this week	Stressors for this week
My break(s) will be on	I won't put myself last for
My social media limit	When I will do my hobby
When I will exercise	I will release anxiety/guilt by

Reflecting on the Week

Something frustrating	Something rewarding

I felt lost when	I felt myself when

I was proud of myself for	I smiled when

I need to let go of	My inner peace level score for this week (1 - 5)

Nothing will ever be perfect, except your love for them.

Monthly Reflection

What was the highest point of the month? Lowest?

Did you remember to say your mantras when you were feeling low?

Do you notice any patterns for when you had negative feelings (triggers, something neglected)?

Do you need to adjust your schedule to give you a better sense of calm?

Go back through the month and reread the third row of each week on the Reflection side. Praise yourself.

Staying Connected

Think about friends and family members you enjoy being around who you haven't been able to spend time with. Make a plan for calling, facetiming, or having a visit.

....
....
....
....
....
....
....
....
....
....
....
....
....
....
....
....
....
....
....
....
....
....

Planning for the Week

My focus for this week	Stressors for this week
My break(s) will be on	I won't put myself last for
My social media limit	When I will do my hobby
When I will exercise	I will release anxiety/guilt by

Reflecting on the Week

Something frustrating	Something rewarding
I felt lost when	I felt myself when
I was proud of myself for	I smiled when
I need to let go of	My inner peace level score for this week: (1 - 5)

Planning for the Week

My focus for this week	Stressors for this week
My break(s) will be on	I won't put myself last for
My social media limit	When I will do my hobby
When I will exercise	I will release anxiety/guilt by

Reflecting on the Week

Something frustrating	Something rewarding
I felt lost when	I felt myself when
I was proud of myself for	I smiled when
I need to let go of	My inner peace level score for this week: (1 - 5)

Planning for the Week

My focus for this week	Stressors for this week

My break(s) will be on	I won't put myself last for

My social media limit	When I will do my hobby

When I will exercise	I will release anxiety/guilt by

Reflecting on the Week

Something frustrating	Something rewarding

I felt lost when	I felt myself when

I was proud of myself for	I smiled when

I need to let go of	My inner peace level score for this week: (1 - 5)

Planning for the Week

My focus for this week	Stressors for this week
My break(s) will be on	I won't put myself last for
My social media limit	When I will do my hobby
When I will exercise	I will release anxiety/guilt by

Reflecting on the Week

Something frustrating	Something rewarding
I felt lost when	I felt myself when
I was proud of myself for	I smiled when
I need to let go of	My inner peace level score for this week: (1 - 5)

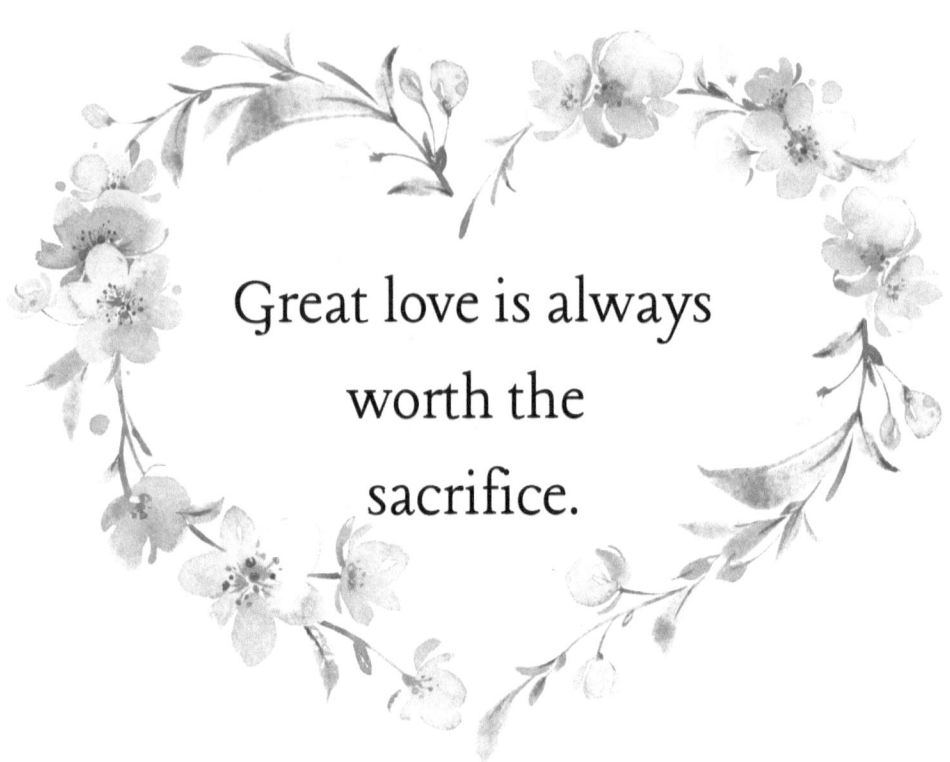

Great love is always worth the sacrifice.

Monthly Reflection

What was the highest point of the month? Lowest?

Did you remember to say your mantras when you were feeling low?

Do you notice any patterns for when you had negative feelings (triggers, something neglected)?

Do you need to adjust your schedule to give you a better sense of calm?

Go back through the month and reread the third row of each week on the Reflection side. Praise yourself.

Think Like a Friend

Start to train your brain to think like a friend. Whenever you have a self-criticism, tell yourself what a friend would say.

Self-criticism	What I Would Say to a Friend

Planning for the Week

My focus for this week	Stressors for this week

My break(s) will be on	I won't put myself last for

My social media limit	When I will do my hobby

When I will exercise	I will release anxiety/guilt by

Reflecting on the Week

Something frustrating	Something rewarding
I felt lost when	I felt myself when
I was proud of myself for	I smiled when
I need to let go of	My inner peace level score for this week: (1 - 5)

Planning for the Week

My focus for this week	Stressors for this week
My break(s) will be on	I won't put myself last for
My social media limit	When I will do my hobby
When I will exercise	I will release anxiety/guilt by

Reflecting on the Week

Something frustrating	Something rewarding
I felt lost when	I felt myself when
I was proud of myself for	I smiled when
I need to let go of	My inner peace level score for this week: (1 - 5)

Planning for the Week

My focus for this week	Stressors for this week
My break(s) will be on	I won't put myself last for
My social media limit	When I will do my hobby
When I will exercise	I will release anxiety/guilt by

Reflecting on the Week

Something frustrating	Something rewarding
I felt lost when	I felt myself when
I was proud of myself for	I smiled when
I need to let go of	My inner peace level score for this week (1 - 5)

Planning for the Week

My focus for this week	Stressors for this week
My break(s) will be on	I won't put myself last for
My social media limit	When I will do my hobby
When I will exercise	I will release anxiety/guilt by

Reflecting on the Week

Something frustrating	Something rewarding
I felt lost when	I felt myself when
I was proud of myself for	I smiled when
I need to let go of	My inner peace level score for this week: (1 - 5)

Nothing moves quite so fast and quite so slow as time.

Monthly Reflection

What was the highest point of the month? Lowest?

Did you remember to say your mantras when you were feeling low?

Do you notice any patterns for when you had negative feelings (triggers, something neglected)?

Do you need to adjust your schedule to give you a better sense of calm?

Go back through the month and reread the third row of each week on the Reflection side. Praise yourself.

Communicate to Change

Think of people in your life who cause you stress. The more you dwell on a bad situation, the more it hurts you. What could you say to the other person to try and improve things?

Try out this format: I feel _(feeling)_ when you _(action)_... because _(reason)_. It would make me feel better if you _(new action)_.

....
....
....
....
....
....
....
....
....
....
....
....
....
....
....
....
....

Planning for the Week

My focus for this week	Stressors for this week
My break(s) will be on	I won't put myself last for
My social media limit	When I will do my hobby
When I will exercise	I will release anxiety/guilt by

Reflecting on the Week

Something frustrating	Something rewarding
I felt lost when	I felt myself when
I was proud of myself for	I smiled when
I need to let go of	My inner peace level score for this week (1 - 5)

Planning for the Week

My focus for this week	Stressors for this week
My break(s) will be on	I won't put myself last for
My social media limit	When I will do my hobby
When I will exercise	I will release anxiety/guilt by

Reflecting on the Week

Something frustrating	Something rewarding

I felt lost when	I felt myself when

I was proud of myself for	I smiled when

I need to let go of	My inner peace level score for this week: (1 - 5)

Planning for the Week

My focus for this week	Stressors for this week
My break(s) will be on	I won't put myself last for
My social media limit	When I will do my hobby
When I will exercise	I will release anxiety/guilt by

Reflecting on the Week

Something frustrating	Something rewarding
I felt lost when	I felt myself when
I was proud of myself for	I smiled when
I need to let go of	My inner peace level score for this week: (1 - 5)

Planning for the Week

My focus for this week	Stressors for this week

My break(s) will be on	I won't put myself last for

My social media limit	When I will do my hobby

When I will exercise	I will release anxiety/guilt by

Reflecting on the Week

| Something frustrating | Something rewarding |

| I felt lost when | I felt myself when |

| I was proud of myself for | I smiled when |

| I need to let go of | My inner peace level score for this week: (1 - 5) |

Teach your children to love themselves by loving yourself.

Monthly Reflection

What was the highest point of the month? Lowest?

Did you remember to say your mantras when you were feeling low?

Do you notice any patterns for when you had negative feelings (triggers, something neglected)?

Do you need to adjust your schedule to give you a better sense of calm?

Go back through the month and reread the third row of each week on the Reflection side. Praise yourself.

Gratefulness

Spend some time thinking of all the things, big and small, that you are grateful for.

Planning for the Week

My focus for this week	Stressors for this week
My break(s) will be on	I won't put myself last for
My social media limit	When I will do my hobby
When I will exercise	I will release anxiety/guilt by

Reflecting on the Week

Something frustrating	Something rewarding
I felt lost when	I felt myself when
I was proud of myself for	I smiled when
I need to let go of	My inner peace level score for this week: (1 - 5)

Planning for the Week

My focus for this week	Stressors for this week
My break(s) will be on	I won't put myself last for
My social media limit	When I will do my hobby
When I will exercise	I will release anxiety/guilt by

Reflecting on the Week

Something frustrating	Something rewarding
I felt lost when	I felt myself when
I was proud of myself for	I smiled when
I need to let go of	My inner peace level score for this week: (1 - 5)

Planning for the Week

My focus for this week	Stressors for this week
My break(s) will be on	I won't put myself last for
My social media limit	When I will do my hobby
When I will exercise	I will release anxiety/guilt by

Reflecting on the Week

Something frustrating	Something rewarding
I felt lost when	I felt myself when
I was proud of myself for	I smiled when
I need to let go of	My inner peace level score for this week: (1 - 5)

Planning for the Week

My focus for this week	Stressors for this week
My break(s) will be on	I won't put myself last for
My social media limit	When I will do my hobby
When I will exercise	I will release anxiety/guilt by

Reflecting on the Week

Something frustrating	Something rewarding

I felt lost when	I felt myself when

I was proud of myself for	I smiled when

I need to let go of	My inner peace level score for this week (1 - 5)

End of Year Reflection

High point of the year: ....
....
....
....

Low point of the year: ....
....
....
....

I am most proud of:
....
....
....
....

How I feel I maintained inner peace: ....
....
....
....

Things I want to try next year: ....
....
....
....

Notes

Other Journals from Orange Blossom

From Burnout to Balance: A Nursing Resilience Journal

Creatives' Journal for Inspiration and Productivity

Teachers' Journal for Balance

The Believer's Journal for Everyday Faith

Mothers' Journal for Inner Peace

Scan here to see the journals and other great books!